Sandra Y. Richter

Persuasive Things

How Internet connectivity can or could change their persuasiveness

Sandra Y. Richter

Persuasive Things

How Internet connectivity can or could change their persuasiveness

GRIN Verlag

Bibliografische Information der Deutschen Nationalbibliothek: Die Deutsche Bibliothek verzeichnet diese Publikation in der Deutschen Nationalbibliografie; detaillierte bibliografische Daten sind im Internet über http://dnb.d-nb.de/ abrufbar.

1. Auflage 2011
Copyright © 2011 GRIN Verlag GmbH
http://www.grin.com
Druck und Bindung: Books on Demand GmbH, Norderstedt Germany
ISBN 978-3-656-09127-1

Persuasive Things

How Internet connectivity can or could change their persuasiveness

SANDRA Y. RICHTER

BERLIN UNIVERSITY OF THE ARTS
COMMUNICATION IN SOCIAL AND ECONOMIC CONTEXT

SANDRA Y. RICHTER
BERLIN, SEPTEMBER 2011

PERSUASIVE THINGS
HOW INTERNET CONNECTIVITY CAN OR COULD CHANGE THEIR PERSUASIVENESS

ABSTRACT

Persuasive technology has the potential to influence user behavior for social benefit. This has been proven to be the case with online games and websites accessible on desktops and smart phones. In recent times, things of everyday life are becoming equipped with technology and are connected to the Internet, an effect which allows persuasive technology to migrate from desktops and smart phones into things of everyday life.

Up until today, only a few Internet connected things have been described in the context of persuasive technology. An extension of theory and frameworks on everyday things is missing. As such, this paper (1) showed how Internet connectivity can or could change the persuasiveness of things, (2) determined which persuasion models fit best to conceptualize and analyze persuasion strategies of such and (3) highlighted which aspects needed to be further incorporated into the models, so that the revised models could be applied to Internet-enabled things. In order to test the persuasion potential of things and the suitability of preexisting approaches, a case of a connected thing promoting physical activity, the Nike+ shoe, was selected and analyzed. The results of this analysis then formed the basis of a new model: The Pervasive Persuasion Model (PPM). Primarily to evaluate the usability of the new model and to guide the direction of its development, the PPM was applied to a connected prototype vehicle that was designed to target behavior change. The trial demonstrated that the concept of the PPM is applicable to a connected thing and can lead to relevant design considerations and concepts. It also suggested analyzing the potential of "persuasion as a value proposition" for connected things.

CONTENT

1. INTRODUCTION

Last year, the CEO of Ericsson, a large provider of communication systems, announced that all things that could benefit from connectivity would be connected to the Internet. He predicted that 50 billion connected non-phone devices would surpass the world's five billion mobile phones in about ten years (Kirkpatrick 2011). Most probably, we will be looking at a lot of smart home applications like dishwashers informing themselves on electricity prices. But what if connectivity goes beyond our electronic devices and enabled our clothing, our cereal boxes and even our shampoo to connect to the Internet?

Equipping things with technology will not only change the objects themselves, but will likely change the people using them. Classically, design can influence a specific behavior often leading to a behavioral change, which may or may not have been intended. The difference now is, that things can interact with the user, and by utilizing a persuasion strategy, can persuade to change the user's behavior intentionally. In order to implement the best such strategies into connected things for social benefit, the concept of persuasive technology should be investigated.

Persuasive technology is a rather new research field describing interactive technologies that motivate and influence users. Approaches on understanding this phenomenon and frameworks on how to build persuasive technology have mainly focused on applications accessible on the computer like websites or games (Oinas-Kukkonen and Tørning 2009). Persuasive things like an interactive flowerpot reminding the user to water the plant are still rather rare, making analysis of these technologies difficult. This is because currently few things of everyday life are technology-equipped and things with Internet-connectivity are even harder to find. However, the migration of technology into things has already begun. Therefore, it is necessary (1) to explore how Internet-connectivity of things can or could change their persuasiveness, (2) which persuasion models fit best to conceptualize and analyze such and (3) which aspects need to be incorporated into the models, in order to extend them to Internet-enabled things. The goal should be to develop an approach for developing and analyzing everyday persuasive things.

Therefore, a background of persuasive technology is presented at first. Structured into three sections, example applications are introduced, the concept of designing for behavior change is outlined and the emerging research field and its origins are described. Drawing on this structure, the next section analyzes an already existing connected thing, a shoe promoting physical activity.

The analysis of the shoe is performed with regard to three acknowledged approaches in the field of persuasive technology. At the end of the section, the different concepts are synthesized and their applicability to the nature of things is evaluated. Utilizing the above findings, a model is developed in the next section. This model addresses the new interaction quality emerging once a thing of everyday life is equipped for tapping into an Internet-enabled network. After presenting the model, it is applied to a current prototype vehicle able to promote physical activity as well.

2. BACKGROUND

As Oinas-Kukkonen and Tørning (2009) emphasize, whenever we communicate with a clear purpose and outcome in mind, we are engaging in an act of persuasion. This is not new. But building machines that engage in persuasion on our behalf is.

According to Fogg (2003), more and more interactive computing systems are designed to change people's behaviors. Therefore, we need to understand how to build and analyze such.

2.1 PERSUASIVE TECHNOLOGY APPLICATION

There are various examples of persuasive technology. Owing to their intent to change behavior, any website or game can be classified as persuasive technology [e.g. book recommendations on Amazon to sell more books, suggestions on who to follow on Twitter to get more users connected, or learning games like Bronkie the Bronchiasaurus, that motivate kids to better manage their asthma (Fogg 2003)]. A variety of similar applications are described in the field of persuasive technology (Persuasive Technology 2006-2010).

More sophisticated uses can be found in technologies like "show-me", a meter that shows how much water has been used in the shower in order to promote water conservation (Kappel and Grechenig 2009), or the "Baby Think it Over Infant Simulator", designed to persuade teens to avoid early pregnancies (manufactured by BTIO Educational Products Inc.), or even the more traditional "Drunk Driving Simulator" (Fogg 2003). These are all interactive computing systems designed to change people's attitudes and behaviors, and can effect positive changes in many areas, like health, business, safety and education. As Lockton et al. (2009) points out, technological advances make consumer products more efficient making users increasingly the weak link in the environmental impact chain. 26-36 percent of household energy use is based on behavioral fail decisions (Lockton et al. 2010). In order to reduce environmental impact, addressing human behavior is paramount and one of the main concerns of designers and theorists in the field. Though, one could also argue that actions like shutting off the light when leaving the house, keeping the apartment at an adequate temperature or sorting trash could all be automated by the technologies themselves. In fact there are now light sensors on the market that turn off the lights when the room is empty.

Health is another area attracting notice. Websites are now adopting persuasive features towards weight loss (Oinas-Kukkonen and Lehto, 2010), giving up smoking (Räisänen, Oinas-Kukkonen, Pahnila 2008), and exercise (Berkovsky et al. 2010) that have all shown signs of success in encouraging people to lead healthy lifestyles. By contrast to sustainability applications, health-related measures cannot be automated and require behavior change which persuasive technology can bring about. Hence the potential of embedded technology in public health should be explored. Clearly, preventive health engineering will be one of the strongest areas for persuasive technology innovation in the near future. For that reason, this paper will focus on embedded technology that addresses health-related issues.

2.2 DESIGNING FOR BEHAVIOR CHANGE

The starting point for the development of a persuasive system is the definition of a target behavior. Fogg (2009a) argues that in order to conceptualize a technology which pursues behavior change, the current and favored behavior have to be defined accurately. Fogg suggests defining both with the behavior grid. The grid differentiates between

- Doing a new behavior, one that is unfamiliar,
- Doing a familiar behavior,
- Increasing behavior intensity or duration,
- Decreasing behavior intensity or duration,
- Or stop doing a behavior.

All target behaviors have a time dimension (schedule). The schedule can either be segmented into doing a behavior one time, for a specific duration, or permanently.

Defining these target behaviors, Fogg (2009a) developed a grid categorizing different types of behavior change by mapping the target with a time dimension (schedule). This leads to 15 different behavior change types enabling a starting point for defining target behaviors.

Fogg (2009a) proposes to cluster research referring to the behavior grid making persuasive applications more comparable. Following this appeal, research published at the "Persuasive Technology" conferences 2007-2009 was organized by behavior type (Fogg and Hreha 2010).

With the grid it is possible to identify, discuss and compare various behavior types and therefore will be considered for the analysis.

2.3 EMERGING RESEARCH FIELD

Technology-mediated persuasion is a rather new research field, which has yet to be further investigated. Persuasive technology combines and overlaps various disciplines through its versatile power and ever increasing complexity. Oinas-Kukkonen and Tørning (2009) explain that mainly areas of human-computer interaction, computer-mediated communication, information systems and affective computing come together in the field of psychology and rhetoric.

The art of persuasion has a long tradition. The power to influence other individuals has always been sought. Persuasion has been studied for centuries, challenging scholars all over the world. In ancient Greece, Aristotle laid the groundwork for rhetoricians and theorists. His work on rhetoric determined the dynamics of how to persuade in any given situation, is yet quoted. The systematical core of Aristotle's work Rhetoric is the axiom that there are three technical means of persuasion: ethos, logos, and pathos. These refer to elements of a speech: speaker, subject treated in the speech, and listener to whom the speech is addressed. These make clear that technical means can only lie within the character of the speaker (ethos), the emotional state of the hearer (pathos) or in the argument (logos) itself (Stanford Encyclopedia of Philosophy 2010).

It wasn't until much later, in 1964 that McGuire set the stage for discussions about resistance to persuasion. He was interested primarily in increasing people's ability to resist unwanted influence. He suggested a theory intertwining personality and persuasion which showed there are people with low or high resistance potential depending on the mediation, the situation and the personality of the person persuaded (The Handbook of Social Psychology 1998).

Predominantly though, the persuasion principles developed by Cialdini first published in 1983, are integrated into today's considerations of persuasive technology. Cialdini (2008) developed six basic social and psychological principles that form the foundation for successful strategies used to achieve influence in the business context: reciprocity (which obligates people to return assistance they may have received from others), commitment and consistency (see also the principle of cognitive dissonance in the Persuasion Handbook 2002), social proof (determining what we think is correct by finding out what other people think is correct), liking (preference to say yes to people we know and like), authority (complying with a request of an authority), and scarcity (assigning more value to opportunities when they are less available). In his work Influence, Cialdini (2008) explains in detail how these principles work and how they can be applied in a business or particularly in a marketing environment.

These principles, frameworks and theories have been useful for understanding the process of persuasion over the past decades and are the basis for all theory on persuasive technology today. Fogg's seminar book (2003) was the first to conceptualize suggestions for software designers, stating, "information technology may play the role of a tool, a medium or a social actor for its users" and is therefore able to persuade. Fogg (2003) defines the union of persuasion and computers as "captology". The three computer functions (tool, medium, social actor) can increase capability, create a relationship or provide experience to make a persuasive affordance possible.

Fogg (2003) also developed 42 principles in regard to the functions of computers learning from persuasion theory drawing conclusions especially from Cialdini.

In 2006 the "First International Conference on Persuasive Technology for Human Well-Being" took place in the Netherlands publishing theories and frameworks in the proceedings (Ijsselsteijn, W. et al., 2006). Since then, "Persuasive Technology" is installed as an annually recurring event where researchers and practitioners meet to present and discuss the development within the field. When studying the proceedings of the different conferences (2006-2010), it shows, that especially theories and practical approaches developed by Fogg but also by Oinas-Kukkonen are frequently quoted and are considered state of the art today. Therefore, an approach of each will be considered for the analysis of a connected thing. Additionally, a third will be selected as explained in the following.

3. ANALYZING CONNECTED THING

In order to evaluate the persuasion potential of an Internet-enabled thing, the persuasive Nike+ application, which is embedded into a shoe, is analyzed with three respected approaches of the persuasive technology field. They are tested and evaluated in regard to their applicability to the nature of things. The findings are summed up in order to draw a conclusion concerning strengths and weaknesses of the approaches.

3.1 SAMPLE CHOICE RATIONALE

Over the past decade there has been a rise in technologies targeting the promotion of a healthy lifestyle, especially physical activity (Consolvo et al. 2009; Lin et al. 2006; Whiteley et al. 2008), but still as of yet, few of these technologies have migrated into things. Beginning to embed technology, there are already more devices tapping into the Internet than people to use them (Evans 2011). Nevertheless, looking for an Internet-enabled thing successfully promoting healthy lifestyles gives very few options.

Regarding to Resatsch (2009), things can be Internet-enabled if they have at least a unique identity, which enables connectivity with resources in a network or even amongst things themselves. Additionally they can have

- Memory capacity, to carry information about the past or future,
- A processing logic for automatic decision processes,
- Sensor technology to collect information about the environment (context awareness),
- A user interface,
- Or a location and tracking possibility, for example at the global level by GPS.

The Nike+ shoe has a unique identity as well as a memory capacity, a location and tracking feature, and can connect to other Internet-ready devices. This makes it eligible for the analysis. Also, the Nike+ application has been studied by Wai and Mortensen (2007) as well as by Segerståhl and Oinas-Kukkonen (2007), which make it a legitimate research subject.

As part of a wider network, Internet-enabled things can interact either directly or indirectly with the user. The degree of interaction is dependant on the features the device itself has. The Nike+ shoe for example cannot communicate with the user directly. It communicates via smart phone, which has a direct connection to the Internet and the user. How this affects its persuasiveness will be considered in the analysis.

3.2 CATEGORIES/QUESTIONS/READING

In order to analyze the shoe, it is determined, what the thing is for, how it interacts with the user and what characterizes it as Internet-enabled. Next, implemented and possible persuasion strategies of the Nike+ application are studied by applying different approaches.

In the field of persuasive technology three approaches for designing persuasive systems receive most attention. A hallmark, the Fogg Behavior Model (2009a) is highly respected in both research and practice, as are most of the concepts developed by Fogg, who, as already mentioned, is a leader in the field. Fogg mainly uses methods from experimental psychology to demonstrate that computers can change people's thoughts and behaviors in predictable ways (Fogg 2011).

Another model was developed by Oinas-Kukkonen and Harjumaa (2009). The model describes how to effectively develop a persuasive system and is more sophisticated than the rather abstract model by Fogg. Due to the technical background of the authors in data processing science, the model focuses more on the information-processing event itself. Though, both models have been applied primarily to computers as persuasive technology. Since the focus of this paper is on persuasive technology migrating into everyday things, a further approach is taken into account: The "Design with Intent" method developed by Lockton et al. (2008). As a scholar in the field of industrial engineering, Lockton was the first to combine design relevant questions with persuasion patterns of technology. Therefore, in the course of the analysis, all three models will be applied to the Nike+ shoe to determine possible and implemented persuasion strategies.

3.3 PERSUASIVENESS OF CONNECTED SHOE

FIGURE 1 NIKE+ SPORT SET, NIKE 2011A

In a society where most people work on a computer behind a desk, it isn't surprising that exercising is becoming more popular. But even though a high percentage of people are motivated to run or do other physical activities, many don't actually exercise on a regular basis. The Nike+ shoe developed by Nike was designed to support users changing their behavior in order to go running more often. Nike sells the Nike+ sport set by promoting it as a two-in-one workout partner and trainer.

The Nike+ sport set (see figure 1) was introduced on May 20, 2006. It measures and records the distance and pace of every walk or run, the elapsed time, and calories burned. This information is then displayed on a screen of a mobile device or broadcasted through headphones motivating the users. This is possible by attaching or embedding a small accelerometer, included in the set, in the running shoe. Once activated, the shoe can be connected with a smart phone (iPhone 3GS or iPhone 4, also possible to connect with iPod but excluded in this analysis). This is a crucial observation in the analysis, as the user interacts only indirectly with the shoe, a point which makes the smart phone part of the research subject. Equally part of the system and therefore of the analysis is the website of the application where running goals can be set and improvement from workout to workout can be monitored.

In order to evaluate the persuasion potential of the system including the shoes, the smart phone application and the website, the three approaches presented are mapped to the case. At the same time, it will be determined to which extent the models are applicable to fit the nature of things and if further elements need to be integrated to evaluate persuasive things.

3.3.1 APPLYING FOGG BEHAVIOR MODEL

In order to evaluate which factors lead to behavior change, Fogg (2009b) developed the Fogg Behavior Model (FBM). The model outlines a systematic approach for designing and analyzing persuasive technology. It illustrates three principle factors, which must be present at the same instant for a target behavior to occur: motivation, ability, and triggers.

The author (Fogg 2009b) states, that, "for a person to perform a target behavior, he or she must (1) be sufficiently motivated, (2) have the ability to perform the behavior, and (3) be triggered to perform the behavior". The Model lends insight to each factor and explains how they are related. According to Fogg (2009b), the location of (potential) users on a xy coordinate depends on the users' level of motivation and ability to perform the target behavior. Both motivation and ability can be increased if they are low. In addition to a high initial value on both axes, the behavior must be triggered appropriately. In short, once the behavior has been triggered, the subject must be sufficiently motivated, be able to perform the behavior, and lastly, be able to associate the trigger with the target behavior (Fogg 2009b).

USER CHOOSES A TARGET BEHAVIOR AND THEREFORE FEELS IN CHARGE

Running is the target behavior of the Nike+ shoe. The + package is marketed as a comprehensive training guide, to support users to be physically active. In choosing what the goal's parameters are (distance, speed, frequency, etc.), the user nevertheless has a measure of freedom choosing the target behavior. **The target behavior** must be set via an interactive interface that can only be accessed by users with a Nike+ account, mobile or at home (see figure 2).

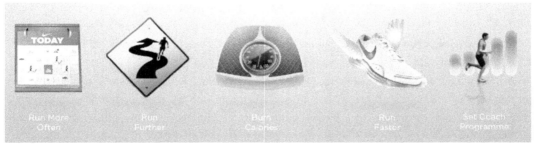

FIGURE 2 GOAL SETTING, NIKE 2011A

Once the goal is set (e.g. run more often or burn more calories), the service suggests specific and measurable tasks (e.g. run four times in two weeks). Depending on the user and his expressed personal goals, the type of behavior change can vary from starting to do a familiar behavior to increasing behavior intensity or duration as for example advanced or professional runners. Since running is a basic activity with few variations for beginners, the behavior change only needs two categorizations (types). Once these types are mapped to the grid it becomes clear that the schedule for both target behaviors is most likely "permanently" (on a regular basis). The target behavior of the Nike+ system is thus twofold: Start to do a familiar behavior, or commit to an increase in behavior intensity.

THE USER IS MOTIVATED THROUGH VARIOUS MESSAGES AND CHANNELS

When a person buys running shoes, a modest, if not high, motivation level must be assumed to exist. Over time, however, the user's motivation level may decrease, with the shoes left forgotten in a closet. Or a person might receive the Nike+ shoes as a gift and doesn't have any motivation to be physically active from the start. In both cases motivation has to be increased.

In order to increase motivation, Fogg (2009b) suggests three core motivators: sensation, anticipation, and social cohesion. Each of these motivators has two sides: pleasure/pain, hope/fear, acceptance/rejection. Fogg (2009b) argues, "The Core Motivators apply to everyone, they are central to the human experience."

Examples of motivators for target behavior in the Nike+ application include pleasure, hope and acceptance elements. Due to the dichotomy of the motivators, the motivation level could also be manipulated more negatively through fear – for example: "You will gain weight if you don't run!" – or through rejection: "Your friends will think you are a loser because you never follow through with anything." The effectiveness of the motivators depends on the user, the context of use, and the user's expressed goal.

FIGURE 3 PERSONALIZED MINI, NIKE 2011A

With a sufficient amount of data, the Nike+ application can build specific motivators (messages) configured to the individual goals and needs of the user. Beyond, Nike implemented the possibility of Facebook or Twitter-connect, which allows for data recovery and data production. In other words, not only can Nike learn more about the user through its partnerships with Facebook and Twitter, but it can also post times and distances on the user's wall or tweetline (e.g. "five km in 20 minutes"), updates which may then increase the user's level of motivation, as friends are free to comment on the user's progress (or lack thereof). Because of privacy issues, few users have allowed the Nike+ application to connect to Facebook, so there is still not enough relevant data on the connectivity features.

In order to ensure motivation even so, Nike created a virtual friend, the "mini" (see figure 3), who comments on the user's progress. The personalized mini can be downloaded as a screen saver sending the user messages to increase motivation. During the run, the music and the mini's feedback are core motivators. Both are not easily integrated into FBM.

CONSIDERING THE ABILITY OF THE USER TIME IS DECIDING

Once a user's motivation level is high, the level of ability needs to be evaluated. Persuasive design relies on simplicity, which increases the ability of a user and can therefore change behavior. In order to develop a simple design, the FBM suggests six interrelated elements: time, money, physical effort, brain cycles, social deviance, and non-routine. Fogg (2009b) explains, "Each person has a different simplicity profile. Some people have more time, some people have more money, and some people pick up things faster, while others cannot. These factors vary by individual and context." Designers and researchers should therefore account for all six elements and identify what users may lack in order to reduce the barriers for performing a target behavior.

In view of Fogg's elements of simplicity for behavior change, the user needs to have a high ability to do target behavior. Most relevant for the Nike+ shoe is the time factor, because running is time-intensive. Before, during and after the exercise, the user needs time, a minimum of an hour altogether. The shoe can't provide a user with time, but it is imaginable that the application for the shoe could be connected to the personal calendar program; sudden changes or free time-slots in the calendar could then be used as a basis for suggesting when a user should train. The feasibility of a calendar feature suggests that the triggers must consider the time factor in any persuasion strategy. At present, however, the Nike+ application cannot be connected to personal calendars.

Also important is the physical effort or, in this case, the physical state of the user (e.g. health issues like weight problems or high heart rate). In general, everyone is able to run (at least for a short distance), but in the interest of health, physical capabilities of each user should be mapped to the shoe for a customized fitness regimen. In order to ensure that the user doesn't run too hard or too lightly, Nike included a heart rate strap which can be connected to the + application (Nike 2011b). If the user's heartbeat is too high, the user is warned. This monitoring feature supports the user's running experience, which leads to positive attitude change.

A further element of simplicity is: making the target behavior a routine. People tend to find behaviors simple if they are routine (Fogg 2009b). Since the target behavior itself is based on routine, it will simplify the behavior change. The development of a routine would also support the target behavior if the Nike+ application were synchronized with the personal calendar of the user. The last three elements of simplicity - money, brain cycle and social deviance - won't affect behavior change to a large degree in this case. Once the Nike+ sport set has been purchased, the user has no additional running costs (monetarily at least); nor can brain cycle or social deviance really be applied in changing a user's behavior or establishing a fitness regiment, since running is a popular, socially acceptable physical activity in most societies. Still, one aspect of the simplicity structure presented by Fogg seems to have been overlooked: technology competence. This aspect is essential for Internet-enabled things, which interact with the user indirectly and are embedded in a multi-device environment, in which the user is obliged to synchronize all of his devices. As Fogg states, each person has a different simplicity profile and is highly context-sensitive (Fogg 2009b). Therefore, the application should be customized for every user.

TRIGGERS ARE ONLY AVAILABLE WITHIN THE APPLICATION

The last factor included in the conceptualization or in research of persuasive technology referring to the FBM is the trigger. The function of triggers is described as sparks, facilitators and signals. Sparks include motivational elements, facilitators make the target behavior easier and signals are well-timed reminders (Fogg 2009b). Depending on the user profile (high/low motivation/ability), different triggers may be used. Triggers are a vital aspect of persuasive products. As yet, Nike has enabled very few triggers to occur outside the application. Therefore, the user has to be rather active checking his online profile for his running information. When implementing the Nike+ application in the user's environment, different triggers can be designed.

Since sparks are designed in tandem with a motivational element, a wide and personalized range of triggers can be sent via e-mail, sms, Facebook or other channels. As Fogg states, "the modality doesn't matter, so long as the trigger is recognized, associated with a target behavior, and presented to users at a moment when they can take action" (Fogg 2009b). Such trigger could take the form of a challenge invitation on Facebook, or a persuasive e-mail motivating the user to go running. Also conceivable is a connection between the user's bathroom scale and the Nike+ application, so once users measure their weight, the application is alerted and beeps as soon as a free slot in the calendar appears arguing with weight gains. This measure may sound radical, but not beyond realm of possibility: a WiFi scale is already on the market by Withings (Withings 2011). Designing facilitators for the shoe has proven to be difficult. As identified in the analysis, time perception is the most important one of all simplicity variables; so time slots can be identified and suggested without using motivational elements. In both cases, a calendar notification is a signal. If the notification becomes a reminder in use (e.g. "10:00 o'clock running in Boston Common") it can be considered a signal. Most triggers occur prior to run and target preexisting behavior. If the user is already in the middle, but should be running faster in accordance with a planned regimen, different triggers will be duly activated (e.g. change of music, voice feedback).

When designing triggers, it should be assumed that, while a user's mobile phone could be a channel for triggering many behaviors, "sparks may also annoy users because they are programmed to motivate us to do something we never intended to do" (Fogg 2009b).

EVALUATING FOGG BEHAVIOR MODEL (FBM) FOR CONNECTED THINGS

The design of the behavior model is simple and therefore easy to comprehend and apply. The consideration that a target behavior can only occur, once a person has both, sufficient motivation and ability, and additionally is triggered to do the target behavior is very plausible. The model is fundamental to understand the persuasion process and is a good starting point for the analysis of an existing persuasive technology or for designing such. The model does not whatsoever present differentiated scales. Rather Fogg (2009b) states, "Sometimes intuition will serve to answer the questions. Other times, designers will need to do primary research with target users. Once designers find the weakness, they can start testing ways to improve this deficient factor."

In order to explore the possible persuasiveness of a connected thing of everyday life it becomes clear that further parameters need to be reviewed. Most important, the thing itself needs to be understood, the use cases have to be defined, and both have to be mapped to the target behavior. Second, the ability for using a thing of everyday life seems to be given and should be evaluated in a large scale to see how this category can be used and complemented with the category "technology competence". For analyzing the motivation the model does not explicitly give guidance and the category remains unclear and too broad to analyze. Except for the three motivators there are no structured evaluation categories, nor are there specific measurable levels of motivation. Additionally, the motivators overlap exceedingly with the consideration of triggers; that is reasonable, but makes the differentiated analysis difficult.

Last, it has to be noted, that the behavior model refers to influencing people's behavior, not attitude (Fogg 2009b). Attitudes become more important when considering things of everyday life.

3.3.2 APPLYING PERSUASIVE SYSTEMS DEVELOPMENT

Oinas-Kukkonen and Harjumaa (2009) developed a framework called the Persuasive System Development (PSD). The framework consists of three steps (see figure 4): understanding key issues of persuasive systems, analyzing the persuasion context (intent, event, and strategy), and the design of system qualities (Oinas-Kukkonen and Harjumaa 2009).

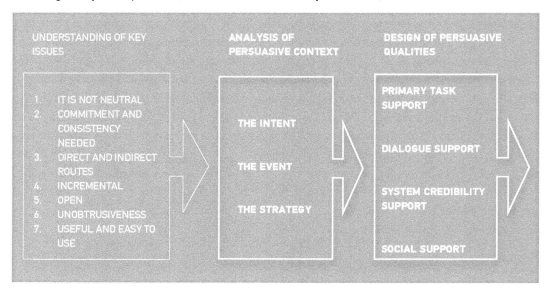

FIGURE 4 PERSUASIVE SYSTEMS DEVELOPMENT, OINAS-KUKKONEN AND HARJUMAA 2009

The first step is based on the recognition of seven postulates which will not be examined since they are implicitly transmitted in this paper. The second step in the PSD model, the persuasion context, comprises elements influencing whether persuasion can take place. The context itself is composed of the intent, event, and strategy and is a core component of the model.

The first building block, the intent, analyses the context of the system designer (the persuader) and deliberates the target behavior (the change type). The change type can be defined by means of the Behavior Grid (Fogg 2009a) as well as the Outcome/Change Design Matrix (Oinas-Kukkonen 2010). Both will affect the design of the persuasive technology.

INTENTIONS ARE NEVER PURE

The intent is characterized by a major publicly traded sportswear and equipment supplier engaging themselves in persuasive technology in order to make it easier for a person to be physically active on a regular basis. Nike' designers embedded arguments in an artifact, the shoe. Their intention is to enter a new business field by selling the Nike+ application and the supplementary gear. The brand Nike+ (which subsumes the Nike+ system) is integrated in the Nike brand to build a strong brand community (more on brand communities see Muniz and O'Guinn 2001). The new product range is both business (selling Nike+ products) and marketing (selling further Nike products). The persuasion target is to support users to do sports on a more regular basis. Nike benefits from a successful persuasion: a stronger brand, more sales and higher revenue. With the persuasive technology and within a gamification approach (more on gamification see Schell 2010) Nike transports their background, culture and values, since "Nike is about bringing what you have to a challenging and constantly evolving game for a healthy lifestyle" (Nike 2011d).

Regarding the change type the goal is to change behavior: run permanently using Nike+ and in the long term changing the attitude to a more healthy and physical active lifestyle. The transformation the software should produce is having fun when doing sports and doing so on a regular basis.

Self-motivation to do sports is difficult for a lot of people and they claim to not have the ability for it for example too little time. With creating the Nike+ application, the company is integrating various persuasive strategies in order to pursue a behavior change and finally a changed attitude. Whether the software system ultimately produces the desired transformation has not yet been proven in a published study. However many users share their experience with the application online. Noone (2009), who blogs at ronisweigh.com about the use of Nike+ says "it just made running so much more entertaining for me. There's something about seeing what you've done, how your pace changes as you go up and down hills, that made me more motivated."

FINDING EVENT PATTERNS IS A CHALLENGE

Describing the event is divided into three context fields: use context, user context and technology context. The use context implies problem domain dependant features, while the user context describes the goals, commitments, compromises, lifestyle, if possible the personality traits of the user. The technology context analyses the features of the technology itself. This part of the building block is highly relevant for analyzing persuasive things since (1) the use case is most probably given, (2) the user context is crucial for the acquaintance, and (3) the technology context is particular once a thing is embedded in an Internet-enabled network.

The use case of the Nike+ shoe is going for a run. Problem-domain dependent features in the form of well-known problems are addressed by the design by including a heart strap measuring heart rate. This prevents the user from exercising too hard which is a typical mistake. Also, the

Nike+ application suggests routes for running which gives the runner assurance regarding the length of the run. A further challenge as mentioned previous, is a high motivation in the beginning, which decreases over time. Especially once the weather gets bad users are less likely to go for a run. Over time more excuses come up and the non-routine (Fogg 2003) will make it harder to resume with the target behavior. These domain dependant issues are to a large degree addressed by the design of the application and already appeared when applying the FBM.

Before analyzing the user context a few words on the concept of grouping users have to be said. The concept of target markets has widely been discussed in the marketing field. Different ideas of how to segment an audience have been published and utilized. Each approach has been criticized in the past arguing that consumers today are less predictable which makes statistic-based targeting difficult. Purchasing patterns no longer neatly align with age and income, and purely demographic segmentation lost the ability to guide a company's marketing decisions. Yankelovich and Meer (2006) published an article in the Harvard Business Review on rediscovering market segmentation. They presented various segmentation types for different purposes all based on data mining, bringing together demographic, behavioral and attitudinal elements (Yankelovich and Meer 2006). Today, this is possible by tapping into the data gathered in the Internet on Facebook and Google in order to develop target profiles going beyond age and occupation, asking which other services customers already use, what they like and so on.

This in mind, it is not an easy question who the users of the Nike+ applications are as a group, especially since the data is not accessible. Basically anyone who can run is able to use the Nike+ application. This results in a divers user group that still has one thing in common: the urge for a healthy lifestyle. Wanting to reduce stress, keeping the body in shape, or just to stay fit could drive this urge. In order to match persuasion to the motivations and needs of the users, focus interviews could be conceptualized to make the application even more user-centered.

The technology context is a lot easier to analyze than the use and user context, building the third element of the persuasion event. The Nike+ shoe is a multiple platform consisting of the sensor-equipped shoe, an Internet-enabled device and a web-based service. The communication with the shoe itself is indirect. Messages and information are sent through the device for example the smart phone. The device is providing music to motivate the user to run. Also, it can give voice feedback or send push notifications. All type of content has a positive appeal suggesting exercise being a game. The approach is through several approximations, rewarding small steps towards changing behavior. This is a specific persuasion quality. In order to understand the strategies of the Nike+ application, the persuasive qualities will be analyzed in the following with the PSD.

THE NIKE+ APPLICATION LEVERAGES WITH A RANGE OF PERSUASION TECHNIQUES

The last building block refers to the message and the route in a persuasive context asking for the form and/or content selected to deliver the intended transformation and for the route direct, indirect, or both (Oinas-Kukkonen and Harjumaa 2009).

Once, the context of the persuasion is outlined, the persuasion strategies can be conceptualized on an operational level. Oinas-Kukkonen and Harjumaa introduced four dimensions that need to be considered when designing or analyzing persuasion qualities (2008, 2010). Each of these addresses an aspect of technology-mediated persuasion. They are relatively well-known persuasive elements within the field of persuasion and persuasive technology and are partially congruent with Fogg's persuasion strategies (Fogg 2003). The elements include primary task support, which addresses the target behavior (e.g. self-monitoring), dialogue support, which deals with the feedback that the system offers (e.g. praise, rewards, reminders or suggestion), system credibility support and social support (e.g. social learning, social comparison, normative influence, competition or recognition), (Oinas-Kukkonen and Harjumaa 2008).

According to the principles of persuasion developed by Cialdini, adapted by Fogg (2003) and refined by Oinas-Kukkonen and Tørning (2009), there are universally valid persuasion techniques. Not all of them are equally powerful. Studying the most used design principles published in "Persuasive Technology" (2006-2008), Oinas-Kukkonen and Tørning (2009) found that tailoring, social comparison, tunneling and reduction have been most applied in the field of persuasive technology. Also, Segerståhl and Oinas-Kukkonen (2007) analyzed various persuasive technology applications with the PSD model. Among the studies, the Nike+ system features were analyzed with the framework for persuasive design, which makes it possible to draw on the findings (Oinas-Kukkonen and Harjumaa 2009).

Regarding primary task support the Nike+ system supports the user by reducing the effort of planning exercises via suggesting scheduled training plans which are categorized according to the runner's goals. This makes it easy for the user. In addition, the user can choose running routes of various distances, which are ranked by other members in the Nike+ community. The system and in particular the community enforces a personalization of the application. Name and picture can be added, the personal mini created (see figure 3). The most highlighted primary task support is the possibility of self-monitoring by tracking the running information (see figure 5). For a lot of users this is the main feature of the Nike+ shoe, as for one user who is quoted in the Wired magazine, "I can log on to Nike+ and see what I've done over the past year," she says. "That's really powerful for me. When I started, I was running shorter and slower. But I can see the progression. I don't have to question what I've done. The data is right there in white and green." (Wired Magazine 2009).

FIGURE 5 RUNNING DATA, NIKE 2011A

The dialogue is supported by various functions integrated in the application. The user receives rewards for personal or group challenges e.g. virtual gifts like badges that can be displayed on the personal profile. In addition to the in-workout audio feedback the user is praised and congratulated by celebrity athletes as Lance Armstrong or Tiger Woods whenever the user achieves a personal best. This feature also gives the application system credibility by simulating expertise behind the system. Also the website (Nike 2011a) states: "Nike+ training programs were exclusively developed by Nike elite trainers for a range of goals and experience levels." It also uses the expression "coach" with its training program offerings. Also, the user can rely on the wisdom of the crowd since running programs are partly user generated and rated by the community. The community at last gives Nike+ social supporting features on many levels. Team challenges or competitions with friends make the application very persuasive. Also the possibility of having a public profile, which shows the user's running data and pictures, allows "social learning by providing means for observing others performing the same behavior and social comparison by offering means for comparing their performance with the performance of others" (Oinas-Kukkonen and Harjumaa 2009).

Not only comparing, also supporting, for example via commenting on a run in real-time or recognition on runs via "likes" on Facebook, can motivate the runner.

EVALUATING PERSUASIVE SYSTEMS DEVELOPMENT FRAMEWORK

The PSD framework is a very elaborate tool in order to analyze a persuasive technology. Taking into account various aspects, it is complex. The PSD model highlights elements which are currently underrepresented as for example the user's personal background and the use situation which have a significant influence on the information processing event (Oinas-Kukkonen and Harjumaa 2008) or the technology context which is particular interesting for connected things. The question arises whether it is possible to develop a use and user context classification for persuasive things and their strategies in dependency of their technological context.

Though, the distinct structure makes it straightforwardly applicable. By including the user in a distinguished manner into the framework, the interaction situation is better understood. Also, it is valuable to explore the strategy with a differentiating view on primary task support, dialogue support, system credibility and social support. These layers make it possible to focus on several elements at a time in order to understand the system in full. Nevertheless, the properties of a thing are difficult to integrate into the framework.

3.3.3 APPLYING DESIGN WITH INTENT METHOD

Lockton et al. (2008, 2009, 2010) established a method useful for designers working on persuasive design of products, services, interfaces or environments. The approach first emerged of the field of Industrial Design Engineering and describes a theoretical model for designing with intent. The Design with Intent method (DwI v.1.0) is a systematic process that supports designers in generating ideas and relevant design concepts for a specific target behavior (Lockton et al. 2010). It was first introduced at the conference "Persuasive Technology 2008" and refers to design intended to influence user behavior across a range of disciplines from architecture to software (Lockton et al. 2008). The method includes 101 patterns for influencing behavior through design, of which each has been tested and developed in a number of variants in workshop sessions with designers (Lockton et al. 2010). The various patterns are grouped into eight lenses according to different kinds of research fields: Architectural, errorproofing, interaction, ludic, perceptual, cognitive, machiavellian and security. These allow designers and theorists to think outside their immediate frame of reference (Lockton et al. 2009).

The architectural lens incorporates concepts developed in the built environment like urban planning and applies them in interaction and product design context; these concepts include material properties, positioning and simplicity. As Lockton et al. (2010) states, "They are effectively about using the structure of systems to influence behavior. Some of the patterns, such as simplicity, feature deletion and hiding things are really fundamental to all kinds of design." These ideas have also been utilized in software applications (like making the "close" button of a pop-up add difficult to find).

Treating deviations from the target behavior is the core of the errorproofing approach, with making errors impossible (or at least difficult) the key strategy. Design can draw on these principles (for example with default settings, or opt-out options of conditional warnings).

The third lens groups all principles that influence interaction and bring together common design elements. Lockton et al. (2010) highlights patterns such as feedback elevations, which often take recognizable form in progress bars and previews. Some of these, like tailoring and tunneling, are identical with the persuasion strategies used by Fogg (2003) and Oinas-Kukkonen and Harjumaa (2009). However, the ludic lens emphasizes techniques for influencing user behavior through a gamification approach. Personal goal setting, competitions and storytelling, as well as unpredictable reinforcement, can be built into an intentional design. Furthermore, the perceptual lens explores perceived patterns and meanings, and enforces color associations, seductive atmospheres, transparency and the broad use of metaphors. On the cognitive level, decision-making processes are important, and heuristics and biases are central. Lockton et al. (2010) included many such patterns now in common use, drawing primarily on Cialdini (among them commitment and consistency, reciprocation and scarcity).

The last two lenses of the Design with Intent method are machiavellian and security, which highlight unethical techniques like degrading performance, slow/no response and surveillance.

All eight lenses borrow from possible persuasion strategies for targeting behavior change in users. In order to develop and analyze things with intent, Lockton et al. conceptualized printed cards of the DwI that make work with all 101-persuasion patterns much easier.

In order to analyze the Nike+ shoe with a method more focused on the thing itself, the Nike+ system will be dissected with the lenses of the DwI method v. 1.0 presented.

The first lens, the architectural, uses the structure of systems to influence behavior. Several of the patterns included in this category are implemented into the Nike+ system (like persuasive material properties). The running shoe is made according to specific running types and users' characteristics for a comfortable fit. The design itself is persuasive and buying a running shoe at Nike.com is likewise. The buying process is tunneled. In just four steps, the user selects gender, surface, arch and stride to find the right gear for the Nike+ system (see figure 6).

GENDER **FEMALE**   SURFACE **ROAD**   YOUR ARCH **MEDIUM**   YOUR STRIDE **NEUTRAL**

FIGURE 6 SELECTED PARAMETERS FOR BUYING A RUNNING SHOE, NIKE 2011B

Once the user's information has been entered, Nike then recommends a shoe to the user. For a woman who runs on roads with a medium arch and a neutral stride, Nike would suggest a design for high performance and low environmental impact, with a mesh upper with synthetic overlays for long-run support, a partial bootie construction for long-lasting comfort, a LunarLite plate

Nike Run Avant+

FIGURE 7 NIKE RUN AVANT+, NIKE 2011B

form at midsole for ultra-lightweight cushioning and adaptive support, and a rubber outsole with deep flex-grooves for flexibility and traction (Nike 2011b). The Nike+ ready shoe is finally complete: The Nike Run Avant+ (see figure 7).

The shoe is now visible on the screen, and with just one click of the mouse, the shopping process can be finalized. In the end, the user will likely have the feeling that the shoe is especially customized; a new relationship between the runner and shoe is forged.

Another pattern borrowed from urban planning is "paving the cow paths". Lockton et al. (2011) describes this pattern as "recognizing the desired paths of some of the users and then codifying them for others." Nike applies this pattern to an extreme extent in the Nike+ system. Nike+ users can see various published routes near home, and find out how often other users in the Nike+ community are running them. The user can choose specific points of interest and select nearby routes. Nike will also suggest specific routes to run based on the personal goals of the user (like burn calories, build lean muscle). This makes running a simple, streamlined activity, since the cognitive intensity required of the user remains low.

FIGURE 8 NIKE SPORT WATCH, NIKE 2011B

Concerning the simplicity pattern, Nike structures the running process in a way that is meant to enable the target behavior. In reference to the DwI method, it ought to be mentioned that the steps of putting on the running shoes, taking the iPhone out and opening the application require very little effort altogether. Though, Nike+ introduced a Nike+ sport watch to make the target behavior even easier to perform (see figure 8). For users who choose to run without their iPhone, it makes the Nike+ shoe even easier to use. The watch can be personalized to show all the data the user wants to see during the run. Afterward, plugged into a computer - via a USB cable - the recorded data can be uploaded, though, features like voice feedback are not accessible.

Considering the errorproofing pattern, (treating deviations from the target behavior as errors, which design can help avoid, either by making it easier for users to work without making errors, or by making errors impossible in the first place), Nike implemented the "Are you sure?" question, which is activated as soon as the runner stops in the middle of a workout. Also, the system warns the user when he or she is going too fast and it can also create tiered challenges, which can only be unlocked when an easier challenge has been successfully met.

The most peculiar errorproofing pattern, though, is making the sensor fit best into the Nike+ enabled shoe. This makes it difficult to use the application with non-Nike shoes.

USING A GAMIFICATION APPROACH TRIGGERS AND MOTIVATES TARGET BEHAVIOR

Social psychology mechanisms like goal setting, or common game elements like scores, levels and collections, can trigger and motivate target behavior. As Lockton et al. (2011) states, "Games are great at engaging people for long periods of time, getting them involved, and, if we put it bluntly, influencing people's behavior through their very design." These mechanisms are heavily used and are a pillar of the Nike+ marketing strategy. As explained prior, users can take part in team- or self-challenges, each with the reward of Nike+ points in return for achieved goals. Collecting and displaying these rewards makes users feel proud about their capabilities.

With a gamification approach, the use of game-play mechanics for non-game applications - particularly consumer-oriented web and mobile sites that encourage people to adopt applications - on Nike+ is becoming stronger due to the implementation of the Nike+ Tag game. After a run, the Nike+ GPS Application user is prompted to play "Tag" (see figure 9). According to Nike (2011c), the user can invite or "Tag" Nike+ friends and email contacts via a customized message that goes out

FIGURE 9 NIKE+ TAG, NIKE 2011C

to friends. The user can set a game of Tag based on distance (person who runs shortest distance is IT), time (person who runs for the shortest amount of time is IT), or order (person to run last is IT). A game of Tag begins when a user first challenges his friends, and ends when the last runner has finished the prearranged Tag route, or at the end of three days, whichever comes first. The Nike+ GPS Application tracks each time a runner is IT and NOT IT, thereby making the running experiences more sporting. This new game of Tag can only be played with the Nike+ GPS application, since the game tracks the runner via GPS data of the phone and not through the shoe, a fact which questions the concept of the Nike+ shoe and will be later broached in the evaluation of the shoe and the suitability of the approaches for analyzing such.

Also implemented are gaps to fill like making suggestions for routes, levels for giving users a feeling of progress, making it a meme via Facebook connect (showing own activity and therefore motivating others or vice versa). A ludic pattern not yet implemented is storytelling, though it's a feature which could easily be incorporated in the application. It is imaginable that going for a run on a specific route tells the user location-based stories and implicitly increases perception.

URBAN AREAS TRANSFORMED INTO PLAYGROUNDS

Seductive atmospherics, through a high density of sensors in urban areas, are possible and foreseeable in the future (Schell 2010). Once these are implemented, they can trigger a specific behavior and be integrated into games (imagine at Starbucks, customers may receive a push notification on their iPhone which invites them to take part in a running challenge or group run, or the challenge of running for Haiti, which was actually launched and is now part of the watermarking pattern). Another possibility could be proximity changes: as soon as a user passes a specific location, the color of his shoe might change or light up. A user's mood may also determine what changes might occur. Changes in color, form or features, as such, have not yet been realized in the Nike+ concept, although lit shoes are not an unknown concept. A further pattern grouped into the ludic perspective worth mentioning is metaphoric. Since metaphors convey concepts (Lackoff and Johnson 1981), they can also convey behavior goals. Nike achieves this by calling its Nike+ shoe a coach.

ETHICAL CONSIDERATIONS ARISE WITH MACHIAVELLIOAN AND SECURITY LENS

Considered unethical, the next lens, the machiavellian, views patterns as acts of degrading performance. The Nike+ system makes full use of these patterns (for example newest features are applicable only with the current device like the iPhone 4). Functional obsolescence in this case would occur if Nike were to develop an upgraded sensor: predictably, a new shoe would have to be designed as well. The shoe itself, as do most trends, will be obsolescent once the latest design of shoes is introduced to the market, a development making the "old" shoe outdated. Also grouped into the machiavellian lens is the freemium model: the first running song is free, but further tracks must be purchased through iTunes.

The security lens describes patterns that are in most circumstances considered unethical. Applying this lens in an analysis makes clear how data is gathered on the users' behavior. Designers may argue about possible customizability and the ability to help users control their own behavior. Features of the monitoring sort are a fraught subject, such as those in the Nike+ system, which combines all possible features: peerveillance through competition and commitment, sousveillance by watching other users, and top-down surveillance by Nike itself.

With such a large user base, Nike is learning things it had never known before. As the magazine Wired (2006) states, "If you enhance your workout with the new Nike+ iPod Sport Kit, you may be making yourself a surveillance target. Nike now knows, in winter, people in the US run more often than those in Europe and Africa, but for shorter distances. The average duration of a run worldwide is 35 minutes, and the most popular running song, which runners can set to give them extra motivation, is "Pump It" by the Black Eyed Peas." Knowing the users is valuable for improving the application and for personalized persuasion (if Nike knows a user likes a specific song, a challenge won could give a similar song for free). But if data is stolen or sold (for instance to an insurance company), it shows: personalization could be problematical.

The interaction and cognitive lens apply patterns presented in the other models; they revert to the fundamental principles developed by Cialdini. As such, they don't need further reiteration.

EVALUATING THE DESIGN WITH INTENT METHOD

As expected, the DwI method brings an entirely new perspective to analyzing a persuasive technology integrated into a thing of everyday life. When applying the architectural lens, questions concerning the design can be readily highlighted. This can close a great gap if one considers applying the FBM and the PSD to the nature of things. Also, the ludic lens is more concrete than, say, the equivalent social support category of the PSD model. It shows how important games in design are nowadays. Game designer Schell (2010) explains, "Games are the next frontier for marketers and advertisers." According to his talk at the DICE in 2010, the psychology behind gamification is grounded in the belief that anything you spend time on or invest money in becomes worthwhile and valuable. That makes it addictive, especially competing in a virtual world with real people and friends. Also Shell (2010) goes on, "Gamification is all about modifying people's behavior." In light of gaming's magnetic draw, the ludic lens should always be considered in the design of a persuasive thing.

All in all, the DwI is a powerful method for designing a persuasive thing. Nevertheless, although the lenses are structured, the analysis and development of the interaction between user and the thing is not. The PSD has a more sophisticated approach in its description of a use context.

As Lockton et al. (2009) puts it, the DwI method is: "A quick method for translating theorists valuable work into practical design suggestions for tackling particular beliefs." The strategies presented consider the design of a product, which the FBM (Fogg 2009b) and the PSD (Oinas-Kukkonen and Harjumaa 2009) don't, and therefore compliments the models well.

3.4 NEED FOR ADAPTED APPROACH

The Nike+ shoe was analyzed regarding its persuasion potential. Especially the fact that the shoe is connected to a network was highlighted when applying the persuasion models to the behavior changing support system. All approaches could be applied easily. The focus of each model was very different so that hardly any replication took place.

The most structured approach is undoubtedly the PSD (Oinas-Kukkonen and Harjumaa 2009). It subsumes all elements of the FBM except the trigger, which could effortlessly be integrated into the PSD. Bringing together the DwI with the PSD is more complex.

Taking the PSD as a starting point, the analysis of the persuasion context (building block two consisting of the intent, the event and the strategy), is singularly useful in its in-depth perception of the persuasion context. Considering the third building block (the persuasion qualities), there are theoretical intersections with the DwI as well as divergences, the latter of which could be narrowed with the method developed by Lockton et al. (2010). The primary task support could be divided into three sections: hardware and software of everyday things as well as their environment including sensors. In addition to the perceptual and errorproofing lenses provided by the DwI, aspects of the architectural lens can be integrated into the analysis or development of primary task support features, though the question of whether these aspects should not rather be integrated into building block two - the technology context directly - cannot be ignored.

Furthermore, dialogue and social support (which basically affects the content and tonality of the message) could easily be merged and brought together with the interaction, cognitive and especially the ludic lens. System credibility however can be brought together with the machiavellian and the security lens, both of which refer to the technology context in total.

This shows that the second building block (the persuasion context) is the most relevant and can be lined with the persuasion qualities as well as the DwI lenses directly. This results in a merged conceptual framework applicable to the nature of things.

Bringing the elements together in detail shows over 100 features; such minutiae is not necessary for further consideration. In order to simplify the aggregated content of all three approaches, one must draw the following conclusion on how to analyze a persuasive thing:

First, the intention as well as the user context must be examined. Secondly, the technology and use context must be considered in order to create hardware and software features for a persuasive thing and its environment (including smart phones etc.). They should be

- Simple to use (drawing on reduction, tunneling, positioning, opt-out mechanisms),
- Customizable (drawing on tailoring, personalization, choice editing),
- Likable (drawing on similarity, social role, material properties, (a) symmetry, metaphors),
- And professional (drawing on system credibility, similarity transparency, security).

Moreover, the messages sent by the technology must be considered. The content of the persuasion message (which can be either emotional or rational) could be one of the following:

- Play with your friends and me (challenges, targets, praise, rewards, levels, scores),
- I help you to do what you want (reminders, suggestions, social support, cooperation),
- I show you what you have done (self-monitoring, simulation, rehearsal),
- I tell you what you should do (normative influence, expert choice framing).

In a persuasive system, messages can appear either in audio, video, text or as images on a device. Basically, every message may be referred to as a trigger, including the last missing part of the three approaches now brought together.

In referring to the nature of connected things, however, two aspects are still missing. First, all three approaches lack a time dimension in reference to the use. There is no guidance whatsoever on how persuasion should be pursued over time. This implies persuasion over a long period of time, but it also suggests the question of how to persuade users before, during and after the use of a persuasive thing. Since such things occupy a place in our lives every day, approaches to design persuasive messages before, during and after the use have to be taken into account. Particularly since connected things are integrated into a complex network, ongoing persuasion is very much possible. Multiple devices enable efficient just in-time interaction with the user, and, as shown, connected things by definition never come into play alone.

This makes one thing very clear: it is not just about persuasive things anymore; it is about persuasive environments made possible by ubiquitous computing. Ubicomp (ubiquitous computing), also referred to as pervasive computing, can be summed up by Resatsch (2010): "Ubicomp is an ubiquitous network and communication infrastructure defined by the presence of various, miniaturized networked, and often invisible technology situated within the range of everyday human actions encompassing applications, supporting interaction, and processes with ease of use." Pervasive computing environments are possible through modern tagging-functions like RFID (Radio Frequency Identification) or NFC (Near Field Communication), basically sensors in general, and microprocessors among advanced technology-integrating things in a network. Interconnected things in combination with smart phones open further fields to possible applications and make it easy for them to be integrated into an Internet-enabled network. This ought to be noted when one analyzes or conceptualizes the technology context.

A further element not fully considered among the different approaches is adaption. Interaction with an Internet-connected thing can be understood as a two-way communication. Once the user reacts, it communicates with the technology that is able to respond to the behavior. The element of tailoring or personalization does not take this into account sufficiently.

Concluding, in order to develop a persuasive thing, it has to be considered part of a network that leads to the possibility of a dynamic-transactional pervasive persuasion. With this in mind, it also shows that the intent (target behavior) should be defined not only as absolute, but over time, such a definition should take into account the phases before, during and after the use of a persuasive thing. Since the three approaches don't include these aspects, a model must be developed which provides a perspective of how to easily apply the merged approaches to things and their pervasive persuasion considering the findings presented.

4. PERVASIVE PERSUASION MODEL

The Pervasive Persuasion Model (PPM) recognizes that human and technology are bound together, continuously interacting and influencing one another. By incorporating time dimension as well as adaption, the model approaches to fit the nature of things interconnected in a pervasive computing environment. In the following sections, the core components of the model are described. The appliance of the model will be theorized, and afterwards applied to test the model.

4.1 ASSERTION OF THE MODEL

The PPM describes the interaction of a user and persuasive technology as a dynamic-transactional process. Once a persuasive thing has its use case, it becomes clear that persuasion takes place before, during and after use. The model consists of two main elements: The user and the artifact system (see figure 10). The elements combine aspects from the approaches presented in the analysis of the shoe; each adds relevant features discussed in the following sections.

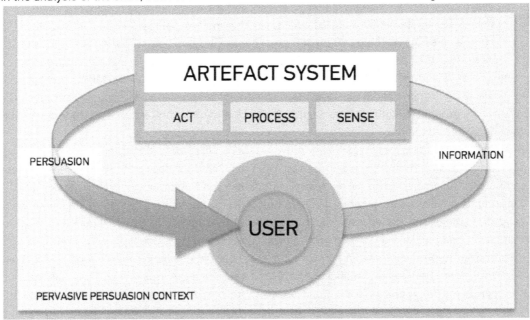

FIGURE 10 THE PERVASIVE PERSUASION MODEL

4.1.1 USER AND USER CONTEXT CAN BE DECODED

Following the model of Fogg (2009b) and Oinas-Kukkonen and Harjumaa (2009), the user and of course his context (symbolized with the circle around the user in the PPM) are two central components of the PPM. Problematic though, is that neither gives guidance on how to analyze the user with any strong degree of precision; this is unfortunate, as not even the most intelligent machines can conduct an analysis without a starting point. Also, as aforementioned, defining groups of people by means of demographic parameters doesn't get us very far. In view of these various limitations, we need a qualitative approach to build pervasive persuasion systems.

Liebl and Rughase (2002) suggest analyzing consumers and their everyday world with a "Storylistening" approach. Listening to the individual destiny of a potential user, we can learn about a specific mindset. The user speaks a collective language which, in turn, can illuminate the behavior of other users with similar mindsets. By listening to potential users and observing their behavior, researchers can build a situational sense of a group that can later lead to discoveries of shared mental patterns among users (like their hidden needs). These insights are valuable when building a persuasive system, or even when evaluating an existing one. If product designer listen carefully to the stories of potential users, they can use the insights for a detailed understanding of the relation between use and meaning of things. Therefore researchers should think of the potential user as a "foreign, exotic tribe which culture has to be studied including its rituals, fetish and interpretation of their world" (Liebl and Rughase 2002). The goal is to learn from the exotic tribe without imposing the own cultural interpretation patterns upon them. This should be done carefully in order to be able to discover the unexpected. Liebl and Rughase (2002) suggest conducting at least ten qualitative interviews to identify patterns. Thereafter, cognitive maps of the interviews can be sketched and brought together to show links. Associations and dedications as well can be captured and brought together in key sentences referring to the cognitive maps developed therefore. With these maps and key sentences, customer segments can be clustered (Liebl and Rughase 2002). These segments can be translated into features of a system, but also into user profiles which can be stored in the system.

Depending on a user's degree of connectedness, information about the user and his context can also be found on the Internet. This information could be matched with profiles stored in the system. Though, Data mining remains difficult, and the creation of algorithms in order to make sense of the data is still a future challenge. A start-up called GraphEffect (2011) is one of the early movers in this field. Their platform allows advertisers to customize Facebook ads by using behavioral characteristics that are not explicitly expressed on the platform. The company mines performance data and allows companies to hyper-target users in a way that Facebook doesn't offer through its advertising platform. For example, based on "likes" and interests, GraphEffect can identify the type of user who might be inclined to buy a product and then target those users. The key is identifying specific traits in order to create what the startup calls "lookalike" models. Personality, motivation and ability may be expressed in data aggregations (Techcrunch 2011).

With this in mind, insights culled from qualitative interviews can be used to build a user's profile. User information on the Internet can further guide programmers on how to shape a personal profile. Processing logic on the Internet can then determine whether a user has a "lookalike" profile already stored in the persuasive system. This seems necessary for having a starting point for persuasion. Thanks to Internet-connectivity, the system may have access to the following kinds of pervasive information:

- User Profile
- Exact location of the user
- Exact time absolute and in regard to the targeted behavior
- Information on the situation including people around him

Further in time, the system can continue learning from each user; the Nike+ system would be a case in point. Ongoing data acquisition can support a company's efforts in persuading the user to change their behavior. The information gathered should be integrated into any system in order to ensure that the persuasion approach suits the user. Likewise, the artifact system should be able to sense and react to information related to the user insights in order for the system to know when to intervene.

4.1.2 ARTIFACT SYSTEMS WILL BE PERVASIVE

Embedded persuasive tools in the built environment, particularly in public or semipublic places, are the future. Sensors will play an increasing role in homes, cities and hospitals. Global players like Cisco, IBM and Microsoft are launching frameworks for cities and working on future solutions (John 2011). By creating intricately linked networks of sensors throughout an urban area, cities are already making great strides toward tracking weather conditions and traffic flow. Seductive atmospherics, through a high density of sensors in urban areas, are possible and foreseeable in the future as well (Schell 2010).

There is no question that sensors can provide all sorts of data, but that data must still be processed by software and analytics in order to yield useful recommendations to interested parties. Storing information in a way that makes it easily and quickly accessible is important too.

Berlin architect J. Mayer H. has won the inaugural "Audi Urban Future Award" with his concept for a city where digital information is continuously exchanged between people, their environment and their cars (see figure 11), but we seem still far away from implementing such visions.

FIGURE 11 A.WAY, MAYER H. J. 2010

Considering the interaction of users with an artifact system designed to persuade, pervasive information must first be sensed, processed and evaluated in order for the system to decide when to act. Some kind of Internet-based system, which would be stored in the cloud and have the ability to read and write, would be necessary to recognize the user's profile and have the capability to sense the user and interact via smart phones or interface-equipped devices.

How it actually sends persuasive messages would depend on the use and technology context (elements of the PSD). The only requirement would be catching the user's attention.

Persuasion can be communicated via design, as well as through audio, video, text or images, while still remaining user-friendly, customizable, likable and professional. These categories are equally applicable for the analysis of a persuasive system: is it simple to use? Can it be customized? Is it likable and professional?

Once a system is triggered, it can then send persuasive messages to users. The idea is to make suggestions at exactly the right time and place, without annoying those who could be persuaded. Now, not only information is pervasive, so are persuasive messages. This is especially important, since persuasion is only initiated by persuasive elements: the actual behavior change is a result of the user's gradual increasing awareness of the importance of that change (Mathew 2005).

Consequently, artifacts literally team up to persuade in a pervasive environment. The messages, as already mentioned, depend on the user and the user context and can be described and implemented in various forms of modalities, such as text, audio, video, feel transporting a user and target specific content. The messages can pursue a supportive or a playful approach with a rational or emotional tonality. Messages depend on what the user wants and needs for example:

- Play a game
- Get support
- Self-Control
- Receive orders

The messages won't be effective if they are just background noise. By contrast, a more sophisticated message can change the user and again, elicit more information. Once the system evaluates how the user acts upon the messages, the system can then draw on the interaction with the user; this process is symbolized with the loop in the model also representing the time aspect.

Regarding to Ijsselsteijn et al. (2006), technology becomes an especially powerful tool when it allows the persuasive techniques to be interactive rather than unilateral (e.g. that is altering and adjusting the pattern of interaction based on the characteristics or actions of the persuaded party, the user's input, needs and context). Also in research, the factor adaptiveness of systems is becoming increasingly prominent. Not coincidentally, personalization is the main topic slated for the conference "Persuasive Technology 2011" (no proceedings available yet). Garzon and Cebulla (2010) argue that model-based personalization, within an adaptable human-machine interface environment, is capable of learning from user interactions. The system can then study which persuasion messages are successful. Algorithmic editing can eventually lead to a highly personalized interaction adapting not only once, but also rather over an extended period.

4.1.3 A NEW QUALITY OF INTERACTION EMERGES

The Pervasive Persuasion Model is not a framework that can throw light on how to conceptualize and implement a persuasive system step by step. Rather, it is a suggestive process for understanding the interaction of users and persuasive systems as ongoing dynamic-transactional processes which can take place anywhere, anytime. It is supposed to support designers and theorists in understanding the interaction, with the end result being the analysis and development of complex systems based on long-term changes in behavior.

Defining the target behavior (also described as the intent) - as Fogg (2009a) argues - should always be the starting point for developing a persuasive system. The PPM suggests supporting behavior change by setting short and long-term goals leading to the target behavior. The goals should be clear in reference to the target behavior, while still taking into account the phases before, during and after the use of a persuasive thing in daily life.

In designing the artifact system and its persuasive messages, the user's motivations, needs, consumption behaviors and patterns first need to be explored. Designers need to emphasize with the user when determining which information is important for the target behavior relative to the target domain like health. Qualitative interviews, diary studies and observations of daily routine can give valuable insights on use patterns, hidden needs and windows of opportunities for interacting directly with the user. These findings play a crucial role in the design of the artifact system. Once the design of the artifact system has begun, the use and the technology context categories (including elements of the Dwl) should be used. Once complete, the strategy, including the message and the route of the persuasion, must be developed next.

Through day-to-day interaction with the artifact system, it must be noted that the system can only react to information it can sense. It is therefore crucial to define which information should trigger the system to persuade the user, and which interface is able to do so at the moment of triggering. In brief, the PPM advises product designers of persuasive things to

- Define a time-dependent target behavior,
- Empathize with the user and his context,
- Extract target behavior relevant information,
- Design an artifacts system with use and technology contexts,
- Conceptualize information sensitive persuasion messages and
- Integrate a learning loop.

The time dimension, and the development of a pervasive artifact system in general, becomes especially interesting when the thing of everyday life can communicate with the user directly, although at present, only a few persuasive Internet-enabled things can communicate directly with the user. Nevertheless in order to test the PPM, an artifact system should include a persuasive thing capable of direct communication (in spite of their relative rarity). This could take the form of a smart fridge or a car with a user interface, although in order to draw on the conclusions of the Nike+ application, a persuasive thing promoting physical activity is more appropriate.

4.2 APPLICATION TO CONNECTED VEHICLE

Physical inactivity is not only caused by an increasingly sedentary work style, but also due to mobility habits, such as the disposition to favor a car or public transportation over walking or cycling. Mobility habits depend on a wide range of variables. One of them is the distance between home and work. The tendency of cities to expand and develop into Megacities most likely lengthens a worker's commute to a degree, which makes walking or cycling almost impossible.

The MIT Changing Places research group has decided to address this issue by creating a persuasive electric vehicle: The Persuasive Electric Vehicle for City Bike Lanes (see figure 12).

The Persuasive Electric Vehicle for City Bike Lanes (PEV) provides energy-efficient mobility and combines the benefits of a bike with those of a car, a union that gives users the freedom to choose between human- and electric power.

The PEV adheres to speed and width regulations of city bike lanes. Besides energy issues, the PEV also

FIGURE 12 PEV, MIT 2011

addresses health related issues that promote physical activity. The designs of the vehicle and driver interface are intended to promote and spur users to exercise and minimize the use of electric power. As Larson et al. (2011) state „For instance, a user could dial in the number of calories they would like to burn during a normal commute home and once they have achieved their cumulative weight goals, the vehicle could provide free electric assistance for commutes to work (so they will not need to sweat)." This makes the PEV not only a thing of everyday life; it is a persuasive thing in terms of this paper.

The PEV will be part of a network able to connect with a GPS-enabled smart phone or other resources. The persuasive thing is therefore considered Internet-enabled. The PEV will have a built-in user interface with a processing logic which makes direct interaction during use possible. Changing Places intends to design and prototype the entire behavior changing support system of the PEV. This includes

- The vehicle and its infrastructure,
- The user interface
- As well as a supporting smart phone application,

All of which are designed to change behavior. The challenge will be to (1) make the PEV mobility option of choice and (2) persuade users to exercise with the PEV via various technology channels before, during, and after a journey. Since the PEV will be available on demand, the phase before the journey warrants especial attention, because physical engagement can only take place once the user chooses to ride the PEV. Therefore the target behavior is: Make the PEV your mobility option of choice and exercise during the ride.

4.2.1 EMPATHIZING WITH A POTENTIAL USER

MIT Changing Places decided to approach three target groups, described as (1) Gen X married with young kids, (2) Baby Boomer Empty Nester and (3) Gen Y Single. Besides age ranges, they are further outlined by life-stage traits, transportation needs and functional needs (see figure 13).

GEN X MARRIED W/ YOUNG KIDS

Age: typically between mid 30's and early 40's
Life-stage traits: family focused, career acceleration, no time to exercise
Transportation needs: car for family trips, low-cost work commuter, personal errands or family trips
Functional needs: low cost, comfort and utility for work and errands

BABY BOOMER EMPTY NESTER

Age: typically 50's-60's
Life-stage traits: seeking new hobbies, established in career, want new way to exercise
Transportation needs: easily accessible, travel with partner, not too physical, easy access and exit
Functional needs: communicate with partner, stay fit, explore landscape

GEN Y SINGLE

Age: typically in 20's and single
Life-stage traits: tech savvy, exploration, want easy way to exercise, large social network
Transportation needs: alternate to public transportation or bike
Functional needs: low cost, ease of access, all weather, comfort and utility for work commuting, social communication

FIGURE 13 MARKETING APPROACH FOR THE PEV, MIT 2011

In order to test the user-centered PPM, a test-subject from the third group, the Gen Y Single, was interviewed. As described in the application method of the model, it is important to empathize with the user. Though it would be preferable to conduct at least ten interviews, as Liebl and Rughase (2002) suggested, in terms of this paper the point can be proven by talking with only one individual who satisfies the demographic and social requirements of the group.

In order to understand his world, the interview is less of a catechism and more of a dialogue about his life, his day, as well as his values, fears and hopes. The goal is to get a sense of how the potential user interacts with his environment on a daily basis. Important too for the interviewer is to inquire about the subject's well-being, health and mobility habits without being too focused on the research interest. Insights from an interview with David, the Gen Y Single, are helpful in describing a random day of a potential user:

"I got up early to go for a run... I try to do this at least three times a week, otherwise my stress level just gets too high. I had a shower at around 10 o'clock. I left the house – too late again. I bought a banana at a corner store before getting on the subway. I was on my way to the dentist's. I took the train up to Alexanderplatz, then changed lines and hopped onto a train towards Friedrichstrasse. Then I changed lines again, took a train to Franzoesische Straße and on the way picked up a cup of coffee to go. Fortunately the train wasn't too crowded. From Franzoesische Strasse, I had to walk for about 10 minutes. I finally arrived at the dentist's and wanted to check in at reception, but the woman at the desk told me my appointment would only be in another week... I was pretty pissed, so to make things better, I called my girlfriend and asked her if she wanted to get a latte at Starbucks. Afterwards, I started to do some work, talked with one of my developers via skype, and tried to salvage the rest of the day.

Around 12 o'clock, I got on the train again to go to the office. I managed to miss my stop because I was absorbed in an article I'd been reading. I then happened to meet a couple of colleagues of mine in front of our office building, and decided to join them for lunch at a nearby cafeteria. I had some very delicious meatballs. On my way back to the office, I had to share an elevator with a guy who reeked. I just thought the day couldn't get any worse.

I conceptualized a focus sheet, had a brainstorming session, skyped with my girlfriend who was having a bad day as well, listened to the presentation of two employees, and then did some paperwork. Later, I called the ADAC, since my BMW Mini showed a flat tire. It turned out it was only a software bug, which kind of made my day. I decided to drive home, but before I went down into the subway to get one of my favorite sweets. There wasn't any traffic, so the drive wasn't too bad, seems like Berlin is empty, not exactly sure why.... Back at home, a friend of ours who was visiting from Vancouver made us dinner, we had friends over and it turned out to be a nice evening. After eating and drinking too much, we went to a nearby Bar met some other friends of ours. At around 2 am we grabbed a cab and drove to a club. The music was great; we danced till dawn and then went back home. What a day."

Already, from this very short dialogue with a potential user, system requirements for a special use case can be inferred. Among others, these observations are noteworthy: (1) getting around a city is part of his day, (2) sport is an important counterbalance to his work life, (3) he likes to read while using public transit, (4) sudden schedule changes are expected and (5) having snacks and good food are highlights of the day. These bits of information may seem very trivial at first glance, but they do contain great importance, as we shall see later.

By checking online profiles on Facebook, or through Google Mail and Calendar, further insights into his life can be gathered; interests in music, movies, favorite locations (accessible with Facebook check-ins), time management: all of it is in the Internet. Also, the location of the Gen Y Single can be found through his GPS enabled smart phone. Data on time, weather is then easily accessed. By collating all of this information, a researcher could build a very good picture of one Gen Y Single, whose personality traits and needs may then be extended to the rest of the target group. Information from multiple sources can be stored and continually updated on one single user ID building a "lookalike" profile.

4.2.2 OUTLINING A PERVASIVE PERSUASION SYSTEM

In order to enable pervasive persuasion (via various technology channels) before, during, and after the journey, an Internet-based system has to be developed which can receive and send information (read and write). It should be directly linked to the vehicle and its environment, to the smart phone via an app, and finally to the desktop device of the user (if possible, with an access to the personal calendar), so it can send outgoing information. It should also be linked with online profiles and any accessible smart environments, particularly those in public or semipublic places that can receive information about the user and the user context (see figure 14).

Building a pervasive Internet-based processing logic that is able to read and write on multiple platforms, accessing and managing users becomes easily possible. In order to create a seamless service, every cog in the chain - from social networks to all user hardware – should be able to be synchronized with others in the cloud.

The service should undertake all PEV related issues and include those that may one day be in fact appropriate. It makes sense to bundle all communication under the umbrella of the PEV, and within target a specific behavior.

FIGURE 14 PERVASIVE PERSUASION OF ELECTRIC VEHICLE

The service must be simple, customizable, likable and professional at all times. As mentioned earlier in this paper, by using the categories of the primary task support described by Oinas-Kukkonen and Harjumaa (2009), the interfaces of the various clients can be conceptualized (e.g. reduction, tunneling and tailoring, including self-monitoring and personalization). Personalization is one of the most important factors in pervasive persuasion: every feature, from software to outward design, should be open to personalization. The object itself represents and forms our identity, so it should lend itself to smart personalization, because to Gen Y Single users, a choice in design is important as it may be to other targeted user groups.

The design of the PEV itself should also be persuasive. Easily added modular extensions, such as personalized color or sound, could be offered as well. In an individualized society that extols the freedom of choice, the addition of a personal feature leads to a stronger relationship between user and things of everyday life. The BMW Mini has been very successful with this strategy, and bicycle providers are likewise following the carmaker's direction. Since the PEV will be an on-demand service, options to personalize the vehicle with colored LED or similar techniques (which are user-adaptable) ought to be considered.

Architectural persuasion must also be well thought-out in the design, as suggested by Lockton et al. (2010); examples of this might include making the button for electric drive harder to find, a twist of convention which might nudge the user to be more physical active.

Each element of the bike, from the wheel and pedal to the charging station, should be analyzed through the architectural lenses offered by Lockton et al. Successful examples of intentional and personalized design can be especially found in other vehicle types, like the car or the bike; since the PEV has included different elements from both transportation vehicles it can learn from developed features.

While the electric vehicle is in use, its interface, which is integrated into the bike, can communicate freely with the user. Text, audio and video formats may jolt the user to deactivate electrical power whenever possible, in order to promote energy-efficiency and physical activity. Instead of having the user snap the smart phone onto a vehicle (as is the case with the electric bike developed by Smart), MIT is planning to integrate the interface into the vehicle as a head-up display (see figure 15).

In order to conceptualize the content and dialogue as well as social support, the categories developed by Oinas-Kukkonen and Harjumaa (2009) can be utilized. Essential are the system's self-monitoring features, which have already been incorporated in the vehicle's concept: "We will

be able to compute energy savings as compared to a typical commuter, CO2 reduction, and health benefits such as calories burned, weight loss, and other key indicators" (MIT 2011).

In theory, the designs of the vehicle's hardware and software will be able to adjust themselves by learning from the user's habits: the pervasiveness of smart-phone technology and other media makes such fine-tuning possible. A corporate design can integrate all clients under a brand umbrella, even at pick-up stations where the PEVs are recharged.

FIGURE 15 PEV INTERFACE, MIT 2011

4.2.3 TELLING A USE CASE STORY

In order to truly empathize with the user and conceptualize in-depth information about persuasion messages, more then one qualitative interview needs to be conducted. The use case of the vehicle must be investigated in greater detail as well. Nevertheless, in drawing on the insights put forth so far, a use case can best be narrated by means of storytelling to demonstrate the resulting design ideas. Stories not only help to understand the users, the product values lies in the details of its interactions and every touch point that a consumer has with it. These can be better explained with telling a story (Doddy 2011).

As a manager of software solutions at Motorola is quoted in the Technology Review (Venkatraman 2011): "Stories allow us to predict, for example, how easily a character such as a tech-savvy 14-year-old-boy can set up our software, and how many choices a schoolteacher mom might want to see in her movie list. Imagining the characters' world helps engineers and designers focus on the most critical features." At Motorola they even invent fictional families giving each character different tastes and interests. Here, in order to draw on the insights on the interview with David, a possible story of a random day of him interacting with the PEV system is told. The story includes considerations of the system and integrates these elements into the short story in the form of a future narrative based in Boston where the PEV is prototyped by the MIT Changing Places research group.

"Two weeks ago, CityRide installed a new kind of e-bikes on my street at 515 Beacon since the Hub Bike Sharing didn't work so well for commuters. I had read about these things in the news, but it was still surprising to see the station near my block. At first, I just walked by. I wondered how much I'd have to pay for a day-pass...

About a week ago, I decided to try one of them out and I was pleasantly surprised. I checked into a bike as a guest user with my iPhone and was able to use the CityCart all day. I drove 'round, did some errands, checked out the electric motor, it didn't feel as dumb as I thought it would. Maybe at the third traffic light, the CityCart asked me how far I needed to go to work each day, and suggested I try out the CityCart the following day to be sure the distance was manageable with support from the electric motor. In the evening I got a message from the CityCart, suggesting I download the CityCart application to make the service easier to use. I downloaded the CityCart app for free. It asked me where I wanted to go tomorrow and calculated how long it would take me. Also, it wanted me sync it with my Facebook account, but I opted not to...

Within the app I saw different in Applications, which made me kind of curious. There was a Farmville and an Angry Bird application, and a Pimp my Body App. Very strange... Though there was also a Gourmet App that I thought I might try out for 79 cents. It recommended a few restaurants in the city too, but...I went to bed and forgot all about it then.

In the morning, my alarm went off and I shuffled into the bathroom. I got into my suit and wasn't so sure anymore if I wanted to take the CityCart and crumple my shirt. It beeped; I had gotten a text from CityRide. It told me there was a great coffee shop on my way to work – well hey, why not. I got on the bike, and it asked me at once if I wanted to listen to the morning news. Very practical. I drove to the coffee shop in flight mode so I wouldn't get my suit dirty and continued on my way to work. On my way back home, I stopped at one of the suggested restaurants to meet some friends. They were all very excited when they saw me on the CityCart.

When I got on the CityCart again, it suggested cross mode, so I even got in some exercise. I guess I could use this service more often. Before going to bed, I received another text from the CityCart, promising that it would send me more café tips. Yummy!"

By telling David's story, features for the PEV can be conveyed. In order to get more insights different situations of David's life can be imagined and visualized. Following the approach of Motorola his family could be made up; stories of an entire city using PEVs could be invented.

Of course, stories of such will not be able to define algorithms or exact system features, nevertheless in order to think through a pervasive interaction situation over and over again, this approach is very helpful.

Besides imagining stories where the user is engaged in the new service, it is also possible to learn from existing applications targeting the same or a similar target behavior especially as suggested the Nike+ shoe (Fogg 2009b). In order to analyze other systems, again, stories of the use of them can be told. Stories are a powerful tool.

At last, it seems important mentioning, that the PEV is a very special example, as it not only targets one behavior (physical activity), but also promotes a second, a sustainable lifestyle. Therefore, also from applications supporting this behavior can be learnt from as for example from the mobile application PerCues (Reitberger et al. 2007) that persuades users to take public mass transportation in order to save fuel leading to a more sustainable behavior.

Conceptualizing one use case narrative can only be a starting point for developing a persuasive thing like the PEV. Also, the prediction, that individual mobility of the future will strongly be linked to the developments of digitally augmented urban spaces, automated driving and personalized data exchange between a human body and its environment transforming a city and its inhabitants into a flow of data should be taken into account.

4.3. EVALUATION OF THE CONCEPT

It showed that the Pervasive Persuasion Model needed to be specific on (1) how to analyze a user, (2) how an artifact system is able to sense a user and his context, and (3) how the system processes and acts upon the sensed information before applying it to a use case. Consequently, the components of the model were explained in great detail and an instruction on how to utilize the model was given. This resulted in a conceptual framework, rather than a model, solely describing the user-technology-interaction as a dynamic-transactional process. This made the PPM applicable to a connected thing: The Persuasive Vehicle for City Bike Lanes.

One aspect, however, which emerged in the application to the connected vehicle, still requires further revision. In the PPM user and artifact system are distinct. The PEV case, though, shows that people and things can instead be described as a collective. The MIT Changing Places group itself actually calls the PEV a human-hybrid (MIT 2011).

In thing theory, Brown (2001) makes a strong distinction between things and objects. He defines objects as distant to the human subject, while things, by contrast, describe less an object and more a particular subject-object relation. Latour (1999) moreover argues that modernity made an artificial ontological distinction between objects and human subjects, whereas in fact it is more accurate to understand both as a hybrid network, a collective of humans and non-humans neither solely natural nor cultural, neither solely unnatural nor unsocial. Böhme (2006) even goes so far as to assert that materiality is still largely confined to the fetish character of things that turns the immaterial inside out. It can be argued that an individual, through the purchase and consumption of goods, places him or herself within a system of signs; things therefore always reflect their users, since they are part of one another.

The synthesis between the user and his things casts a particular light on the double role of technology, which is, on the one hand, a part of the human, but on the other hand, also emancipated enough to have its own "will". Therefore, the PPM should be reevaluated if one accepts that the user and its things cannot be thought of as separate units. Included into these considerations shall be the question if and how the relationship of people and things change once the things are connected to the Internet.

Nevertheless, the approach of storylistening has shown to be a valuable method for developing hypothetical interactions between a user and his/her persuasive thing. The model has proven to support such conclusions by introducing an ongoing loop of interaction before, during and after the use of a persuasive thing over time engaged in an Internet-enabled pervasive network.

5. CONCLUSION & FUTURE WORK

Although technology migration into our things of everyday life has already begun, we are far from the predicted 50 billion connected non-phone devices. So far even, that it was difficult to find an Internet connected thing with a measurable level of persuasiveness. Nevertheless, the discovery of the Nike+ shoe as one such example provided insights into how persuasive a thing can be once it's integrated into an interactive network.

The analysis of the connected shoe was carried out with applying respected models of the persuasive technology field. The models of (1) Fogg, (2) Oinas-Kukkonen and Harjumaa, and (3) Lockton' et al. uncovered the persuasion potential and the concrete strategies of the connected shoe. At the same time, strengths and weaknesses of the approaches could be discovered. By drawing on these findings, a new concept was developed: the Pervasive Persuasion Model (PPM).

The PPM highlights the observation that the persuasion potential of things truly unfolds when the things are integrated into a pervasive network - here referred to as an artifact system – that is able to sense, process and act through various technology channels at all times. The smart phone within seems to take over an important role and might even soon become the most powerful channel for persuasion (Fogg and Eckles 2007).

The dynamic-transactional perspective of the new model addressed the interaction quality that emerges once a thing is tapped into an Internet-enabled network. The concepts of storylistening and storytelling were introduced to make the persuasion model a stronger basis for the conceptualization and analysis of persuasive things. The model could then be applied to a current prototype vehicle with a design that encourages users to be physically active.

By considering the utilized approaches first ideas for the artifact system of the Persuasive Vehicle for City Bike Lanes could be developed.

Features for the connected vehicle were conceptualized based on the perception of a user's story. These indicated that a user can benefit from the persuasiveness of a thing promoting physical activity, and that persuasion can possibly be the central value proposition of such a product.

Further research will determine if, and to what extent, persuasion can be included in the business model of a connected thing. In order to do this the Persuasive Vehicle for City Bike Lanes will be considered. Therefore, more interviews with Gen Y Singles must be held in order to better analyze value creation, delivery and capture of the persuasion.

On the basis of this paper's findings, stronger persuasion strategies for the PEV can be developed and later tested to determine their potential. Outside the Gen Y Singles, further target groups should be considered to verify the functionality of the user-centered Persuasive Persuasion Model. After the realization of this research, the model shall be revised and applied to future cases and domains.

"Digital technology will conquer the cities. In the intelligent, sensor-controlled cities of the future, the interaction of people and sensors will shape not only work and leisure, but also traffic. Cities will have much more intelligent and faster traffic systems than today, as the different components will be better harmonized with each other. The boundaries between individual transport and means of public transport will be fluid, and machines will adapt themselves to our needs – not vice versa."
Prof. Carlo Ratti 2011

. BIBLIOGRAPHY

Räisänen, T., Oinas-Kukkonen, H. and Pahnila, S., 2008. Finding Kairos in Quitting Smoking: Smokers' Perceptions of Warning Pictures. In: H. Oinas-Kukkonen and et al. (eds). 2008. Persuasive Technology. Berlin: Springer, pp. 254-257.

De Kort, Y. et al., 2007. Persuasive Technology, Second International Conference on Persuasive Technology, Persuasive 2007. Berlin: Springer.

Berkovsky, S. et al., 2010. Physical activity motivating games: virtual rewards for real activity. CHI 2010, pp. 243-252.

Böhme, H., 2006. Fetischismus und Kultur. Eine andere Theorie der Moderne. Hamburg: Rowohlt Taschenbuch Verlag.

Brown, B., 2001. Thing Theory. [online] Available at: <http://faculty.virginia.edu/theorygroup/docs/brown.thing-theory.2001.pdf>[Accessed 29 August 2011].

Chatterjee, S. and Dev, P., 2009. Persuasive Technology, Fourth International Conference on Persuasive Technology, Persuasive 2009. Claremont, CA.

Christof, R., 2010. Aristotle's Rhetoric. In: E. N. Zalta (ed.). 2010. The Stanford Encyclopedia of Philosophy [online] Available at: <http://plato.stanford.edu/archives/spr2010/entries/aristotle-rhetoric/>[Accessed 10 August 2011].

Cialdini, R., 2008. Influence: Science and Practice (5th Edition). New Jersey, NJ: Prentice Hall.

Evans, D., 2011. The Internet of Things. [online] Available at: < http://blogs.cisco.com/news/the-internet-of-things-infographic/>[Accessed 29 August 2011].

Consolvo, S. et al., 2009. Goal-setting considerations for persuasive technologies that encourage physical activity. In: S. Chatterjee and P. Dev (eds). 2009. Persuasive Technology. Claremont, CA.

Dillard, J. P. and Pfau, M., 2002. The Persuasion Handbook: Developments in Theory and Practice. Thousand Oaks, CA: Sage Publications.

Doody, S., 2011. Why we need storytellers at the heart of product development, UX Magazine. [online] Available at: <http://uxmag.com/strategy/why-we-need-storytellers-at-the-heart-of-product-development>[Accessed 29 August 2011].

Fogg, B. J., 2011. Peace Innovation Lab @ Stanford University. [online] Available at: <http://stanfordpeaceinnovationlab.org/team/>[Accessed 29 August 2011].

Fogg, B. J. and Hreha, J., 2010. Behavior Wizard: A Method for Matching Target Behaviors with Solutions. In: T. Ploug, P. Hasle, and H. Oinas-Kukkonen (eds.). 2010. Persuasive Technology. Berlin: Springer, pp.117-131.

Fogg, B. J., 2003. Persuasive Technology: Using Computers to Change What We Think and Do. San Francisco, CA: Morgan Kaufmann.

Fogg, B. J., 2009b. A Behavior Model for Persuasive Design. In: S. Chatterjee and P. Dev (eds). 2009. Persuasive Technology. Claremont, CA.

Fogg, B.J. and Eckles, D., 2007. Mobile Persuasion: 20 Perspectives on the Future of Behavior Change. Stanford, CA: Stanford Captology Media.

Fogg, B.J., 2009a. The Behavior Grid: 35 Ways Behavior Can Change. In: S. Chatterjee and P. Dev (eds). 2009. Persuasive Technology. Claremont, CA.

Garzon, S. R. and Cebulla, M., 2010. Model-Based Personalization within an Adaptable Human-Machine Interface Environment that is Capable of Learning from User Interactions. In: R. Jarvis and C. Dini (eds.). 2010. ACHI 2010, pp. 191-198.

Gilbert, D. T., Fiske, S. T. and Lindzey G., 1998. The Handbook of Social Psychology (4th Edition). New York, NY: Oxford University Press.

Graph Effect, 2011. Your brand on facebook. [online] Available at: <http://grapheffect.com/ge/index.html>[Accessed 3 July 2011].

Ijsselsteijn, W. et al., 2006. Persuasive technology for Human Well-Being: Setting the Scene. In: Ijsselsteijn, W. et al. (eds.), 2006. Persuasive Technology. Berlin: Springer, pp. 1-6.

J. MAYER H, 2010. J Mayer H's A.WAY Concept Wins Audi Urban Future Award. [online] Available at:<http://www.bustler.net/index.php/article/j_mayer_hs_a.way_concept_wins_audi_urban_futur e_award/>[Accessed 29 August 2011].

Kappel, K. and Grechenig, T., 2009. "show-me": water consumption at a glance to promote water conservation in the shower. In: S. Chatterjee and P. Dev (eds). 2009. Persuasive Technology. Claremont, CA.

Kirkpatrick, M., 2011. How 50 Billion Connected Devices Could Transform Brand Marketing & Everyday Life. Read Write Web Blog. [online] Available at: <http://www.readwriteweb.com/archives/how_50_billion_connected_devices_could_transform brand_marketing_everyday_life.php>[Accessed 3 July 2011].

Lackoff, G. and Johnson, M., 1981. Metaphors We Live By. Chicago, IL: University of Chicago Press.

Larson, K. et al., 2011. Application for Support from the MIT Energy Initiative [MITEI] Seed Fund Program. [leaflet] March 2011 ed. MIT: Changing Places Research Group.

Latour, B., 1999. Pandora's Hope. Essays on the Reality of Science Studies. Cambridge: Harvard University Press.

Liebl, F. and Rughase, O. G., 2002. Storylistening, GDI Impulse. [online] Available at: <http://www.sr-partners.com/html/pdf/storylistening.pdf>[Accessed 29 August 2011].

Lin, J.J., et al., 2006. Fish'n'Steps: Encouraging Physical Activity with an Interactive Computer Game. In: P. Dourish, A. Friday (eds.), 2006. UbiComp 2006. Berlin: Springer, pp. 261–278.

Lockton, D. et al., 2008. Design with Intent: Persuasive Technology in a Wider Context. In: H. Oinas-Kukkonen and et al. (eds). 2008. Persuasive Technology. Berlin: Springer, pp. 274-279.

Lockton, D. et al., 2009. Influencing Interaction: Development of the Design with Intent Method. In: S. Chatterjee and P. Dev (eds). 2009. Persuasive Technology. Claremont, CA.

33

Lockton, D. et al., 2010. Design with Intent: 101 Patterns for Influencing Behavior through Design v.1.0. Windsor: Equifine.

Mathew, A. P., 2005. Using the Environment as an Interactive Interface to Motivate Positive Behavior Change in a Subway Station. In: G. Van der Veer and C. Gale (eds.) 2005. CHI '05 Extended Abstracts on Human Factors in Computing Systems, pp. 1637–1640.

McClusky, M., 2009. The Nike Experiment: How the Shoe Giant Unleashed the Power of Personal Metrics, Wired Magazine. [online] Available at: <http://www.wired.com/medtech/health/magazine/17-07/lbnp_nike>[Accessed 3 July 2011].

Muñiz, A. M. and O'Guinn, T. C., 2001. Brand Community. Journal of Consumer Research, 27(4), pp. 412-431.

Newitz, A., 2006. Nike+ Ipod = Surveillance, Wired Magazine. [online] Available at: <http://www.wired.com/science/discoveries/news/2006/11/72202>[Accessed 21 July 2011].

Nike, 2011b. Nike products. [online] Available at: <http://nikerunning.nike.com/nikeos/p/nikeplus/en_EMEA/products> Accessed 21 July 2011].

Nike, 2011c. TAG! You're IT Tag game. [online] Available at: <http://inside.nike.com/blogs/nikerunning_reporter-en_US/2011/01/21/tag-you-re-it> Accessed 21 July 2011].

Nike, 2011d. Annual Report. [online] Available at: <http://media.corporate-ir.net/media_files/irol/10/100529/nike2011ar/nike2011ar/index.html#mark_parker_letter/> [Accessed 21 August 2011].

Nike, 2011a. What is Nike+. [online] Available at: <http://nikerunning.nike.com/nikeos/p/nikeplus/en_EMEA/plus/#//dashboard/>[Accessed 21 July 2011].

Noone, V., 2009. My Running Partner – The iPod/Nike+, Ronis Weigh Blog. [online] Available at: < http://ronisweigh.com/2009/03/my-running-partner-the-ipodnike.html>[Accessed 3 July 2011].

Oinas-Kukkonen, H. and Lehto, T., 2010. Persuasive Features in Six Weight Loss Websites: A Qualitative Evaluation. In: T. Ploug, P. Hasle, and H. Oinas-Kukkonen (eds.). 2010. Persuasive Technology. Berlin: Springer, pp. 162-173.

Oinas-Kukkonen, H. and Harjumaa, M. A., 2008. A Systematic Framework for Designing and Evaluating Persuasive Systems. In: H. Oinas-Kukkonen and et al. (eds). 2008. Persuasive Technology. Berlin: Springer, pp.164-176.

Oinas-Kukkonen, H. and Harjumaa, M., 2009. Persuasive Systems Design: Key Issues, Process Model, and System Features. Communications of the Association for Information Systems, 24(28), pp. 485-500.

Oinas-Kukkonen, H. and Tørning, K., 2009. Persuasive System Design: State of the Art and Future Directions. In: S. Chatterjee and P. Dev (eds). 2009. Persuasive Technology. Claremont, CA.

Oinas-Kukkonen, H. et al., 2008. Persuasive Technology, Third International Conference on Persuasive Technology, Persuasive Technology. Berlin: Springer.

Oinas-Kukkonen, H., 2010. Behavior Change Support Systems: A Research Model and Agenda. In: T. Ploug, P. Hasle, and H. Oinas-Kukkonen (eds.). 2010. Persuasive Technology. Berlin: Springer, pp. 4-14.

Ploug, T., Hasle, P. and Oinas-Kukkonen, H., 2010. Persuasive Technology, Fifth International Conference on Persuasive Technology, Persuasive Technology. Berlin: Springer.

Ijsselsteijn, W. et al., 2006. Persuasive Technology, First International Conference on Persuasive Technology, Persuasive Technology. Berlin: Springer.

Rao, L., 2011. GraphEffect Launches Intelligent Facebook Advertising And Targeting Platform For Brands, Techcrunch. [online] Available at: <http://techcrunch.com/2011/08/19/grapheffect-launches-intelligent-Facebook-advertising-and-targeting-platform-for-brands/> [Accessed 21 August 2011].

Reitberger, W. et al., 2007. The Percues Framework and its Application for Sustainable Mobility. In: Y. de Kort et al.l (eds.). 2007. Persuasive Technology. Berlin: Springer, pp. 92-95.

Resatsch, F., 2010. Ubiquitous Computing. Wiesbaden: Gabler.

Schell, J., 2010. When Games Invade Real Life. [video online] Available at: <http://www.ted.com/talks/jesse_schell_when_games_invade_real_life.html>[Accessed 28 July 2011].

Segerståhl, K. and Oinas-Kukkonen, H., 2007. Distributed User Experience in Persuasive Technology Environments. In: Y. de Kort et al.l (eds.). 2007. Persuasive Technology. Berlin: Springer, pp.80-91.

Venkatraman, V., 2011. The Storyteller, Technology Review. [online] Available at: <http://www.technologyreview.com/article/38273/>[Accessed 2 September 2011].

Wai, C. and Mortensen, P., 2007. Persuasive Technologies should be Boring. In: Y. de Kort et al.l (eds.). 2007. Persuasive 2007. Berlin: Springer, pp. 96-100.

Whiteley, J., et al., 2008. State of the Art Reviews: Using the Internet to Promote Physical Activity and Healthy Eating in Youth. American Journal of Lifestyle Medicine, 2(2), pp. 159–177.

Withings, 2011. The WiFi Bodyscale. [online] Available at: <http://www.withings.com/en/bodyscale>[Accessed 2 September 2011].

Yankelovich, D. and Meer, D., 2006. Rediscovering Market Segmentation. Harvard Business Review. [online] Available at: <http://hbr.org/product/rediscovering-market-segmentation/an/R0602G-PDF-ENG> [Accessed 3 August 2011].

www.ingramcontent.com/pod-product-compliance
Lightning Source LLC
LaVergne TN
LVHW082349060326
832902LV00017B/2732